Seven Powers of One Word

Transforming Adversity into Destiny

Seven Powers of One Word

Transforming Adversity into Destiny

SUSAN M BROWN

Seven Powers of One Word

© 2015 by Susan M. Brown

All rights reserved. No part of this publication may be reproduced, stored in a retrieval system, or transmitted in any form or by any means—for example, electronic, photocopy, recording – without the prior written permission of the author. The only exception is brief quotations in printed reviews.

Unless otherwise indicated, Scripture quotations are taken from the New King James Version, Copyright©1962 by Thomas Nelson, Inc. Used by permission. All rights reserved.

Scripture quotations marked (NIV) are taken from the Holy Bible, New International Version®, NIV®. Copyright © 1973, 1978, 1984, 2011 by Biblica, Inc.™ Used by permission of Zondervan. All rights reserved worldwide. www.zondervan.com

Library of Congress Control Number: 2015917803

ISBN: 978-0-9969435-0-5

Printed in the United States of America

Dedication

I dedicate this book to my mom for instilling the love for words and books deep within my heart and to my three most precious children, Kristen, Andrea and Colin for trusting me with your hearts and for being immensely forgiving, loving and patient while I learned how to use the power of my words.

Acknowledgments

To Colleen, Cheryl, Karen, Laurie and Shelley – Thank you for all you did to heal my heart and strengthen my faith.

To Donna Lang – Thank you for your strategic vision for my business and challenging me to think outside of the box regarding the power of one word.

To Jai Stone – Thank you for calling forth my authentic best self and believing in my work. I would not have written this book without your faith in me and in the seven powers of one word.

To Lisa Plato – Thank you for creatively articulating one of the five saboteurs with your "stray dog" metaphor and for every time you graciously rescued me when I needed creative direction and insight.

To Kathy Stoltzfus – Thank you for your transformational coaching that helped reveal my calling and the theme of this book.

To Tony Stoltzfus – Thank you for your body of work that transformed my heart and the soul of my business.

To Bonnie Ross Parker – Thank you for being a source of inspiration to live life fully and for being my #1 advocate for all I do.

To Tracy Lawson Hobbs – Thank you for initiating me into the power of one word. Who knew that your gift of kindness, the tiny blue stone laid upon my doorstep, would open the door to my destiny?

Hardship often prepares an ordinary person for an extraordinary destiny.

~ C.S. Lewis

Contents

1	Introduction	1
2	Overview of the Seven Powers of One Word	9
3	Discover Your One Word	13
4	Power to Organize	23
5	Power to Nourish	29
6	Power to Energize	35
7	Power to Waken to the Miraculous	41
8	Power to Optimize	49
9	Power to Realign	55
10	Power to Define	61
11	Five Saboteurs and Twelve Activation Strategies	67
12	Five Stages of Influence	77
	About the Author	85

CHAPTER 1
Introduction

Every adversity, every failure, every heartache carries with it the seed of an equal or greater benefit.
~ Napoleon Hill

Seven days before Christmas, I felt a lump in my breast. After my doctor examined me, he immediately ordered a biopsy, increasing my anxiety. On December 27, I was terrified when I found out I had breast cancer. During the time of year, known as the season of hope, I had little.

My diagnosis plunged me into a dark void, a fear-driven free fall. I dreaded telling our five, seven and nine-year old children that I had breast cancer. When my husband and I broke the news to them, our five-year old asked, "Mommy, are you going to die?" Her question increased my determination to hide my fear to minimize theirs. That was easier said than done. Thoughts of dying haunted me by day and at night, twisted my dreams into nightmares. While I slept, I battled threats like a raging fire, overpowering waves and murderous intruders. My deep-seated anxiety intensified the rising tide of hopelessness.

Drowning emotionally, I grasped at lifelines. I gathered survival statistics, adjusted my diet, exercised, met with other survivors, prayed sporadically and occasionally, took anti-anxiety medication. Each strategy only temporarily subdued my hopelessness. However, I wanted to permanently conquer it.

A few days after I shared my feeling of hopelessness with a friend, she inadvertently gifted me with the lifeline that would change my life. She left a tiny blue rock inscribed with the word, hope, on my doorstep. That one word became the lifeline tethering me to my destiny.

From a scientific perspective, hope set up a positive dialogue between my brain and body. Medical research from the field of psychoneuroimmunology shows that our thoughts release molecules of emotion that adjust the chemistry of our body, influencing our health. Our beliefs and expectations – critical components of hope - are important triggers that release good or bad chemicals throughout our brain and body. These chemicals block pain, encourage healing and help repair the damaging effects of fear and stress.

In Scripture, hope is a strong and confident expectation about the future and the manifestation of things yet unseen. It is dynamic, active, directive and life sustaining. Hope converts you from victim to victor, giving you the energy and confidence to fight for your future. My one word carried the colossal promise that God is my rock of refuge and the giver of hope.

Needing constant reassurance of that promise, I kept my rock with me, hidden in my purse or pocket, and even slept with it under my pillow. As my hope grew, so did my faith in the power of one word. My word had uprooted my fear, the pesticide poisoning my thoughts. Hafiz, a Sufi poet, underscores the power of words to build a healthy mental and emotional foundation. He says, "The words you speak become the house you live in." My one word helped build an emotional and spiritual shelter in which I could thrive. With hope in hand, I took command of my destiny.

You, too, possess the power to direct your destiny. That power is never more available than when adversity disrupts your life. Traumatizing events like illness, death, divorce, betrayal, financial setback or job loss detonate your life, shattering your comfort zone. As the ground beneath your feet explodes, seeds of destiny are released. Those seeds must be cultivated to survive an atmosphere of fear.

Fear is your enemy, a destructive force that sabotages the fulfillment of your divine potential. Fear is

Introduction

a paralyzing force, creating helplessness. Fear seduces you to stay within the confines of your comfort zone, a false shelter.

Our natural instinct is to treat fear as an enemy, reacting in one of three ways. One option is to hold your ground and fight against the source of your fear. A second response is to freeze, paralyzed as a deer caught in the headlights. A third reaction is to run away from the source of your fear. However, you have one more choice, one rarely chosen.

The fourth option is to plunge into your fear, aided by faith and courage. I saw this happen when my twenty-three-year-old daughter made her first bungee jump. Terrified and trembling, with a bungee cord coiled around her ankles, she inched her body into position atop a three-foot platform. She stood alone, suspended 500 feet above a ravine in New Zealand, without a safety net. When the guide gave the signal to jump, she let out a terrifying scream as she dove headfirst into her fear.

As she safely bounced up and down on her life-saving cord, she wore the triumphant smile of a conqueror. Rather than fight, flee or freeze, she courageously surrendered to her fear, strengthening her character and resiliency.

Washington Irving noted, "There is in every woman's heart a spark of heavenly fire, which lies dormant in the broad daylight of prosperity, but which kindles up and beams and blazes in the dark hour of adversity." Cancer ignited my spark and hope fueled the blaze, transforming my adversity into blessings. In fact, one year after my final round of chemo, I wrote a letter of gratitude to cancer for how it had helped deepen my faith, reduce my perfectionism, increase my peace and appreciation for the beauty of life, strengthen my family and bring me into the presence of God.

Over the past four years, I have shared the power of one word with hundreds of individuals, associations and faith-based organizations, teaching them how to use it as a transformational tool in the midst of adversity. During this time, seven unique powers of one word emerged.

Introduction

In the chapters ahead, you will discover how to direct your destiny by tapping into each of the seven powers of one word. Power, used in this context, is a guiding force that holds the potential to influence your thoughts, feelings and actions and unearth your divine potential. In chapter two, I provide an overview of the seven powers using the acronym, O.N.E.W.O.R.D. In chapter three, I share my proven process for discovering the one word that is best for you given your current circumstances, challenges and goals. In chapters four through ten, I reveal how each power works by sharing my clients' results along with the science and scripture that underwrite each power. In chapter eleven, I expose the five saboteurs that diminish or destroy your word's power along with twelve strategies to activate and maximize the power of your word. In the final chapter, you discover how to increase your influence and impact with the help of your word.

Your destiny is a journey, taken one step and one word at a time. There is one word right now, resting in your heart, waiting to be discovered. The people around you need your one word, released through you, to help them come alive and break free from their limitations.

CHAPTER 2

Overview of the Seven Powers of One Word

*As long as we are persistent in our pursuit of our deepest destiny, we will continue to grow.
We cannot choose the day or time when we will fully bloom. It happens in its own time.*
~ Denis Waitley

Picture a seed no larger than a period turning into a 60-foot, 4600-pound, 200 year-old cactus. This miracle of nature is the rare Saguaro cactus found only in the Sonoran Desert. Remarkably, at ten years of age, it is a mere one and a half inches tall! This black speck challenges your imaginative abilities as well as your faith to trust that something so small carries such tremendous growth potential.

My faith in the power of one word grew slowly, not unlike the Saguaro cactus. During my battle with cancer, I did not fully appreciate how my word, hope, would impact my life. At that point, I was years away from discovering its seven powers. As a result, I forgot about my one word lifeline for ten years. My interest was reignited by a blog about how to use one word to replace your New Year's resolutions. What I read immediately resonated with me, taking me back in time when hope had transformed my life.

Aware that I was a living testimony to the power of one word, I was eager to share this easy, success tool with others. Drawing from my years of teaching, I created "Power of One Word" workshops. My earliest workshops presented one word as a guiding force, an inspirational vitamin, a fresh lens by which to view life and an excavation tool to unearth your potential. However, as new powers burst forth, the value of one word grew; much like the Saguaro cactus sprouts new limbs. The acronym, O.N.E.W.O.R.D. represents the seven powers: Organize, Nourish, Energize, Waken, Optimize, Realign, and Define.

Where one person may activate four of the seven powers, another may use only one or two powers. For example, a client diagnosed with breast cancer chose the word, believe, which <u>nourished</u> her spirit, <u>energized</u> her to write an e-book and <u>wakened</u> her to the miraculous. The word, unparalleled, helped another client <u>optimize</u> her resources and <u>realign</u> her priorities to grow her business.

Your one word also contains five stages of influence that begin with an understanding of its power to transform adversity into destiny and end with your having authority over your word to benefit others. In chapter twelve, I detail each stage.

Just as the magnificent 4600-pound Saguaro cactus lays hidden beneath the harsh desert environment, the weight of your destiny and your future impact is contained within the seed of your adversity. Your one word contains unlimited growth potential, released and ignited by your desire to fulfill your destiny. While you cannot dictate when you will bloom, you can choose the day you plant your seed.

CHAPTER 3
Discover Your One Word

The difference between the right word and the almost right word is the difference between lightning and a lightning bug.
~ Mark Twain

It is vital to choose the best word, the one that holds lightning level voltage, to receive maximum benefit. How do you find the right word?

You explore what lies within your heart by specifically listening to your heart's desires. Your deepest desires are your fundamental motivations impacting your actions, thoughts and beliefs. Your desires, especially the unmet ones, create a restless void that wants to be filled. Tony Stoltzfus, author of *The Invitation*, explains, "Most of the crazy, twisted stuff we do that causes us so much pain is aimed at filling these unmet desires with things in this world." The role of your heart in determining your destiny cannot be understated. "If we would see the color of our future, we must look for it in our present; if we would gaze on the star of our destiny, we must look for it in our hearts." (Canon Farrar)

Moving into the heart, King Solomon, known as the wisest man offers this caution, "Keep your heart with all vigilance, for from it flow the springs of life" (*Proverbs 4:23*). The condition of our heart determines whether we create a life of stagnancy, disease or poverty or one that reflects growth, health and abundance.

While it might appear risky to seek your heart's guidance, you are at greater risk by not consulting it. Your heart has been implanted with God-given desires that enhance your life when fulfilled in healthy, moral and legal ways. When you fulfill your desires in healthy ways, you move closer to your destiny. Your heart always directs you, whether or not you are listening to it.

As you are considering possible word choices, notice whether you have chosen a word to please someone else. If so, this is a red flag. Your one word takes on the negative energy of guilt when you use "should" and resentment when you use "have" to. Both word choices send the message to yourself that you are "not enough," increasing your resistance to your one word. Words fueled by guilt or shame lower your motivation, energy and enthusiasm. You diminish the power of your word if you use it as a tool to manipulate or impress others or as a way to fix your past behaviors.

Your heart contains one word jam-packed with unlimited power to transform your challenges into a strengthening of your character or capacity, moving you towards your destiny. Each exercise invites you to listen for the whispers of your heart. Find a comfortable place to relax, without distraction.

You may want to play soft music, pray, meditate or breathe deeply to declutter your mind to hear the soft, still voice of God and engage your heart's intuition. Complete the exercises until you find the one word that is best for you at this time.

1. Ask yourself the question: Whom do I most admire and why?

Your person or character can be living or dead, real or fictional. Pinpoint the top one or two qualities you admire. If you are missing one of those qualities, notice if your heart yearns to develop that quality. If not, it is natural to admire the traits of others without the need to integrate their qualities into your character.

Years ago, the Disney character, *Pocahontas,* inspired me to choose bold as my word. I loved how she consulted Grandfather Tree for his wisdom and guidance. I especially resonated with her spiritual nature, desire for growth and her boldness to face her unknown future.

2. Read over the list of 16 God-given heart desires below compiled by Tony Stoltzfus. (Listed in *The Invitation*, page 88). Circle words that evoke a strong emotion.

Joy	Security
Love	Goodness
Comfort	Peace
Challenge	Approval
Significance	Worth
Belonging	Come Through
Justice	Achievement
Be Known	Recognition

Next, find synonyms for each of your circled words. This step helps you choose the word that most resonates with you. For example, if your heart seeks significance, but that word does not resonate with you, consider other words like excellence, leadership or destiny. Choose the one word that feels biggest to you or generates the highest enthusiasm. It is natural to even feel a little fear because the word may seem a bit out of your reach.

3. Images contain the power to evoke strong feelings and help uncover your heart's desires. An image of a rock climber may trigger your desire for adventure, challenge or achievement while making you feel strong and confident. Look for images online, in magazines or books or use the resources listed below to find three to five images that evoke strong feelings, negative or positive.

As you look at each image, ask:
Which of my heart's desires does this image trigger?
Is it time for me to focus on this desire(s)?

If this is your time to focus on a desire you named, search for a word that best reflects what you really want. In my workshops, people often are drawn to the image of a person reclining in a hammock at the beach. It triggers positive feelings for those reminded of a fun and relaxing vacation.

For others, it represents the unmet desire for peace. As a result, people chose words like fun, rest, peace, self-care and balance.

Note: I also use a set of 216 images at www.ccl.org and 32 images at www.coach22.com.

4. Ask yourself one or more of these key questions:

> What is missing in my life? (Consider the following areas: career, finances, health, spirituality, relationships, family, recreation and fun)
>
> What word do I want others to use to describe me?
>
> What word or need feels bigger than me? (Look at a desire, dream, or goal that seems unattainable)
>
> What do I want to share with others?

> What do I need to fulfill my destiny, legacy or purpose?

Record or take note of what you hear, sense or see. That information will reveal the one word that is best for you right now. Anna, in the next chapter, chose valor. She sensed that her word felt impossible to achieve. She also knew her word would conquer her fear, transforming her life.

5. Make a list of ten negatives in your life that you are tolerating and would like to change. Invite God to reveal what He has for you instead of the negative. Make a list of those promises. Your one word may be one of the promises, pointing you towards your destiny.

Trust your instincts, the whispers of your heart and other signs leading you to your one word. Working with a sales team of twenty people, I asked each person to keep track of words that raised or lowered their energy from the images or words spoken by others. One woman, a self-proclaimed perfectionist, shared her list of twenty-five words. She asked how to narrow her list down, no simple task for a perfectionist! I noticed how one word was starred and when I asked for an explanation, she had no idea why she had done that. I speculated that divine guidance might have been at work. With a grin, she confirmed she had discovered the perfect word for her!

Once you have your one word, it is time to activate one or more of the seven powers and avoid sabotaging its influence. In chapters three through nine, I share the scientific and faith-based secrets behind each of the seven powers. Once you understand how each power works, you gain confidence in your one word's ability to direct your destiny.

CHAPTER 4
Power to Organize

Let a man restore order within himself,
and chaos without ceases.
~ Christian Nestell Bovee

When I met Anna, her life was a self-proclaimed mess. Being married to an abusive, alcoholic and unemployed husband stole her confidence and courage. Anna was emotionally exhausted and living in fear. Her spouse had turned into a man she no longer recognized and she prepared herself for divorce. While Anna welcomed the peace divorce offered, she was not ready for the upheaval it would cause in the lives of her two young children. The fear of the unknown paralyzed her, preventing her from making decisions.

Anna's topmost desire was to restore order to her chaotic emotions and lifestyle. Knowing she also needed to conquer her paralyzing fear, she chose the word, valor. She shifted her focus from her fear-fueled present to a courage-driven future. Consequently, she made empowering decisions that reduced her internal and external chaos. As insignificant as this may appear, Anna enrolled in an exercise class that she had avoided taking due to her fragile body image. She also searched for a new home and remarkably, found the house of her dreams. Anna envisioned hanging a beautiful sign out front that read "Valor Farm." She pictured her home as "being a safe, serene place for anyone to gather that needed to be empowered to let their courage shine!" Both decisions reflected her newly organized and confident inner state.

It is easy to maintain order when Plan A is working. However, adversity collaborating with chaos, creates confusion in both your internal and external environments. Your one word holds the power to remove the veil of confusion, re-establishing order.

Scientific Fact

Millions of bits of sensory data from your physical environment bombard your system in every waking moment. Your conscious mind is equipped to handle approximately 130 pieces of information per second out of the millions of stimuli present in your environment. Thankfully, your Reticular Activating System (RAS) filters the incoming data. The RAS takes instructions from your conscious mind about what is important to notice and then that information moves into your subconscious for current or future use.

How does your mind decide so quickly?

Your attitude, emotions and expectations dictate the focus of your RAS. Think of your RAS as a "bouncer" that sits at the door of your mind. Imagine yourself after a busy and stressful day, sitting in a crowded restaurant. Will you notice the friendly conversations, soothing music or delicious aromas? Or, will you focus upon the kitchen noises, a couple arguing or displeasing artwork?

Your one word, when properly activated, goes into your subconscious activating your RAS to filter incoming data that relates to your one word. When Anna activated valor, she noticed opportunities, people, and choices related to courage that would have otherwise gone undetected. One word organizes the millions of stimuli to bring order to your internal and external chaos.

Spiritual Truth

"Now the earth was formless and empty, darkness was over the surface of the deep, and the Spirit of God was hovering over the waters. And God said, 'Let there be light,' and there was light." *Genesis 1:2-3*

Power to Organize

The Spirit of God was waiting in the wings to bring order to the formless and empty void. His command for structure and order was succinct as God looked at the darkness. He transformed the chaotic state into a complex, organized universe with the key word, light.

Scripture also reveals how God created something from nothing by His one word and by faith. "By faith we understand that the worlds were prepared by the word of God, so that what is seen was made from things that are not visible" *(Hebrews 11:3)*. God's one word declaration carries creative and organizing power which is made available to us: "Truly I tell you, if you say to this mountain, 'Be taken up and thrown into the sea,' and if you do not doubt in your heart, but believe that what you say will come to pass, it will be done for you" *(Mark 11:23)*. Your one word, activated by faith, carries the potential to order your reality.

**Daily Questions to Activate
the Power to Organize**

Increase order and organization in your heart, mind and spirit as well as in your living and work environments. Choose one or more questions to start your day. Include your word or a form of your word in each blank. Ask the question out loud once and allow your subconscious to work on your behalf.

How can _____ help organize or stabilize my thoughts and/or emotions?

How does _____ want to help me organize my time and energy better?

What is _____ showing me about chaos or disorganization?

CHAPTER 5
Power to Nourish

Words are, of course, the most powerful
drug used by mankind.
~ Rudyard Kipling

When Patty was twelve years old, her mom passed away from breast cancer and within five years, her father died from emphysema, leaving her an orphan. As an adult, she had not fully resolved her childhood trauma. At forty-seven-years-old and a mother to her twelve-year-old son and seventeen-year-old daughter, she was terrified of dying before her next birthday.

The thought of leaving her children without a mom gnawed at her happiness. Her fear was stealing her joy of being a mom.

Patty chose the word, trust, to fulfill her heart's desire for security, peace and joy. Three weeks later in what seemed like a cruel test to the power of her one word; Patty was diagnosed with breast cancer. Her fear of dying was now more real than ever as she prepared for a double mastectomy.

She grabbed trust as I had gripped hope. Her lifeline nourished her spirit and realigned her priorities. With trust in hand, Patty created a blog for her online supporters entitled *Another Chapter in Life....Trusting God*.

Scientific Fact

In *Words Can Change Your Brain,* authors Andrew Newberg and Mark Robert Waldman state, "A single word has the power to influence the expression of genes that regulate physical and emotional stress." A single word holds the power to release dozens of stress-producing hormones and neurotransmitters, hindering your immune system and interrupting brain functioning. If placed into an fMRI scanner and the word NO is flashed for less than a second, you would see a sudden release of stress chemicals into your brain. In fact, just seeing a list of negative words for a few seconds will make a highly anxious or depressed person feel worse. The more you dwell upon negative words; you impair structures that regulate your memory, sleep, appetite, emotions, feelings and your brain's ability to regulate your happiness, longevity and health.

Alternatively, words like hope, peace, trust, and joy nourish your body at the cellular level by releasing hormones like serotonin that induce a healthy internal environment. When adversity enters your life, choose words that increase your faith, optimism and peace vs fear, despair and insecurity. In doing so, you generate health-inducing chemicals to increase your sense of safety and well-being, interrupting the amygdala's fight or flight reaction to real or imagined threats.

Spiritual Truth

"If you put these instructions before the brothers and sisters, you will be a good servant of Christ Jesus, nourished on the words of the faith and of the sound teaching that you have followed" (1 Tim. 4:6, NRSV).

The Bible describes itself as spiritual food using words like water, milk, bread, and meat. In Matthew 4:4, we find that when Satan tempted Jesus to turn stones into bread, He said His word was even more important to our well-being than actual food. "It is written, man shall not live by bread alone, but by every word that proceedeth out of the mouth of God."

Your one word is an inspirational vitamin, a source of nourishment to yourself and others. Proverbs 16:24 says, "Pleasant words are as a honeycomb, sweet to the soul, and health to the bones."

Daily Questions to Activate the Power to Nourish

Insert your one word or a form of your word into one or more of the questions. Begin each day by asking one or more questions.

God, how will _____ provide nourishment today?

Why does _____ easily feed my spirit?

How can I demonstrate _____ today to refresh my spirit?

CHAPTER 6
Power to Energize

Your destiny is to fulfill those things upon which you focus most intently. So choose to keep your focus on that which is truly magnificent, beautiful, uplifting and joyful. Your life is always moving toward something.
~ Ralph Marston

Carol was exhausted from caring for her 92 year-old mother and managing both of their households while running her startup business. She was determined to find a word to increase her waning energy. Carol's logic told her to find a "strong and powerful action word."

As you read earlier, it is vital to consult your heart to find your one word. As Carol discovered, it is common for your logical reasons to clash with heart messages. During the word-finding exercises, Carol's heart told her to pick the word, cherish. Her logic rebelled by calling it "soft and weak." Despite her doubts, she stuck with cherish and four months later sent me an update on how her one word had transformed her life.

> "For the last few years I have been 'chasing the money,' trying to keep two households going. If I only worked hard enough, I thought that 'someday' I would be able to make enough money to take her to Hawaii and the Grand Canyon, have help around the house, and give lavishly to the charities of her choice on her behalf, etc. What dawned on me, was how I was missing opportunities with Mom RIGHT NOW and we might not have the luxury of a 'someday.' I re-prioritized

by putting God and my mother first, cut back on the time spent outside the home and paid attention to all the small joys of everyday life. I consciously cherish my time with Mom, seeking ways to make each day fulfilling for her.

Carol's word helped her increase her energy by doing four things differently: 1) live a life of purpose and meaning; 2) build the habit of practicing gratitude; 3) realign her actions with her priorities; and 4) reorient her focus from living for the future to being fully alive in the present.

Scientific Fact

All that is seen and unseen has energy. David Bohm, a renowned physicist wrote, "The universe is a sea of energy." Even our emotions have energy. David Hawkins, the author of *Power vs Force,* developed a scale calibrating our emotions to different levels of energy. For example, he notes that bliss, serenity and reverence are in the upper ranges of energy while despair, anxiety and humiliation are low in energy. Newberg and Waldman found that if you concentrate on a word like peace or love, you raise your energy by calming the emotional centers in the brain, reducing anxiety and depression.

Your one word sends off a "vibe" according to Dr. Judith Orloff, the author of *Emotional Freedom*. She goes on to explain how "words set off a love bomb or a noxious explosion" and "transfers energy to the target, eliciting a response." Your one word holds the potential to increase or decrease the spiritual, emotional and physical reservoirs of energy in yourself and others.

Spiritual Truth

Scripture uses the word, quicken, to explain how words in the Bible can impact our energy when facing adversity. Psalm 119:107 says, "I am afflicted very much: quicken me, O Lord, according unto thy word." Quicken is a Biblical Greek word meaning to "make alive, give life or vitality" (Strongs #2227). If your spirit is quickened while reading scripture, you receive a deeply personal message causing you to feel invigorated, energized, moved, inspired, animated or excited. A quickened word is a seed implanted in your spirit, releasing uplifting energy.

Daily Questions to Activate the Power to Energize

Increase mental, physical, emotional and spiritual energy by placing your one word into the blank in each question. Choose one or more questions to start your day.

When I place _____ in my heart, what do I sense, hear or feel from God?

If _____ could talk, what does it want me to increase or reduce in my life?

When I think of _____ as a seed, how can I water it today?

CHAPTER 7
Power to Waken to the Miraculous

Expectancy is the atmosphere for miracles.
~ Edwin Louis Cole

At twelve years old, Pamela turned to drugs to numb her pain. Three different men had sexually abused her for four years, beginning when she was just five years old. Twenty-seven years old and unmarried, she tried to commit suicide after she lost custody of her three-year-old son. She was also beaten, choked, raped and incarcerated eight times on drug-related charges. Pamela was no stranger to adversity or miracles.

Pamela shares that she experienced the miraculous healing power of God's Word while in prison. "I had a relentless desire to change and I only began to heal after I started memorizing scripture every day," she told me. When we met, Pamela had just completed her third year of being drug-free and was now the founder of Chebar Ministries, a nonprofit that restores the lives of women released from prison.

Pamela was restless for more healing, believing "her best was yet to come." She wanted to overcome her low self-worth caused by years of abuse. Pamela wanted to find a way to stop sabotaging her happiness and level of impact. She attended my workshop, intrigued by the power of just one word to change adversity into destiny. She fully expected her new word to deliver a miracle, another healing with no rational explanation.

Pamela chose the word, significance, setting her miracle in motion. She describes what happened, "My word has really opened my eyes to see that I do have worth, that I have purpose and walk in His divine plan today. Significance gave me the ability to receive the freedom, which alone came from God. There was no way I could do that on my own." Her miracles continue as she is currently working with an author and two movie producers to have her story told.

Scientific Fact

We turn to the field of quantum physics, which studies the unseen realm to make sense of the physical realm and explain remarkable events. The logical part of our brain demands explanations for things like spontaneous remissions, experiments where an observer alters reality, psychokinesis where thoughts bend metal objects like forks, and the placebo effect where our beliefs change our biological response to disease. Max Planck, the founder of quantum theory, conducted research that concluded all matter is made of energy fields making it a simmering field of potential, constantly creating itself in ways that are stranger than we can imagine.

Neurologist Allan J. Hamilton as quoted on Harvard Medical School's website says, "What, I wondered, should those of us in the medical field do with such unsettling disturbances, such seeming ripples of the supernatural? Ignore them? Or should we declare them simply to be a puzzling mixture of science and spirit? Can we now allow ourselves to entertain the possibility that the supernatural, the divine and the magical may all underlie our physical world?"

You can use the power or energy of your one word coupled with your strong beliefs to influence or cause an event that defies your logic and current understanding of the laws of nature.

Spiritual Truth

Every dead and hopeless place in our lives is waiting for a wake-up call, a spoken and powerful word, to alter our circumstance and/or our character. There is arguably no greater miraculous wake-up call than the one Lazarus received.

Mary, the sister of Lazarus, sent word to Jesus to come and heal a dying Lazarus. Jesus delays and when he arrives Lazarus has been dead for four days, properly buried in a cave. Jesus and others go to the cave where John reports, "And when he thus had spoken, he cried with a loud voice, 'Lazarus, come forth.' And he that was dead came forth, bound hand and foot with graveclothes: and his face was bound about with a napkin. Jesus saith unto them, loose him, and let him go" (*John 11:43-44*).

In several other instances, Jesus uses powerful words to waken those around him to the realm of miracles. He cast out a fever (Luke 4:39), commanded the sea to be still (Mark 4:39), cleansed a leper (Mark 1:41-42), and removed hearing and speech impediments (Mark 7:34-35).

Your word, spoken in faith, cultivates the soil from which miracles spring. "And Jesus said unto them, Because of your unbelief: for verily I say unto you, If ye have faith as a grain of mustard seed, ye shall say unto this mountain, Remove hence to yonder place; and it shall remove; and nothing shall be impossible unto you" (*Matthew 17:20*). Your certainty lies not in how God redeems your adversity, but in His promise to do it. "And we know that all things work together for good to them that love God, to them who are the called according to his purpose" (*Romans 8:28*).

Daily Questions to Activate the Power to Waken

Maximize the power of your one word to waken the miraculous by placing your word in each of the blanks. Begin each day by asking one or more questions.

God, how will _____ be used today to increase my faith in your unsurpassed power?

What part of me wants to be wakened by my one word, _____?

God, what is on your agenda today with _____?

CHAPTER 8
Power to Optimize

*You cannot be anything you want to be –
but you can be a lot more of who you already are.*
~ Tom Rath

The United States Army Rangers are the best-trained, combat-ready soldiers in the world. They are mentally and physically tough and highly prepared to fight our country's adversaries. Quincy, a former Ranger and decorated officer was used to being in control in hostile surroundings. That changed when he entered civilian life and became the manager of an inner city retail store.

Quincy described his work environment as "harsh." He was overwhelmed by constant negativity, unmotivated and underperforming employees and long hours. Quincy was at a career crossroads wondering if he should quit. However, his primary goal was to ensure that his decision aligned with God's will.

As we explored his options, Quincy also prayed for guidance. He got a definitive answer, which was to remain in his current position. Quincy responded by releasing his resistance to his situation and committed to developing key leadership traits to become a man of excellence. He also sought ways to shift from a lifestyle of surviving to thriving.

Quincy wanted a word to optimize his time, energy, talents and resources. He chose sangfroid, a French word meaning "composure or coolness, sometimes excessive, as shown in danger or under trying circumstances." Quincy enhanced the skills he had used in the army to handle pressure and adversity. No longer rattled, he took his leadership to the next level. Quincy optimized his communication strategies and implemented innovative and supportive employee programs. He began to thrive in his urban combat zone. Within nine months, Quincy received the Outstanding Leadership Award at the NAACP Image Awards.

Scientific Fact

Gallup scientists have studied human potential for over forty years. After extensive research involving more than ten million people, they concluded that people magnify their potential for growth when they focus on developing their strengths instead of remediating their weaknesses. Additionally, they found that those who do this are more than three times as likely to report having an "excellent quality of life." (*Strengthsfinder 2.0* by Tom Rath).

When you choose to optimize strengths that deeply matter, you increase your emotional buy-in. As a result, your resistance to change decreases and your determination to use your one word increases, enhancing your results.

Spiritual Truth

Therefore, my beloved, be steadfast, immovable, always excelling in the work of the Lord, because you know that in the Lord your labor is not in vain.
1 Corinthians 15:58

The Greek word for excel, *perisseuo,* means "to be abundantly furnished with, to have in abundance, abound in (a thing), to excel more than, to exceed." Scripture provides three key reasons for us to excel.

The first reason is to glorify God. "Let your light so shine before men, that they may see your good works and glorify your Father in heaven" (*Matthew 5:16*).

The second reason is to build your character and spiritual maturity through the pursuit of excellence. "Finally, brothers, we instructed you how to live in order to please God, as in fact you are living. Now we ask you and urge you in the Lord Jesus to do this more and more excel" (*1 Thessalonians 4:1*).

Lastly, God uses your excellence to influence the world around you. Nehemiah, whom God called to rebuild the walls of Jerusalem, demonstrated a strong commitment to completing his mission with excellence. Nehemiah faced constant opposition from his enemy, Sanballat. While atop the wall, Nehemiah responded to the distractions by repeatedly saying, "I am doing a great work and cannot come down" (*Nehemiah 6:3*). The purpose for optimizing your strengths is for the good of others.

Daily Questions to Activate the Power to Optimize

Maximize the potential of your one word to bring out the best in yourself by placing your one word into the blank in each question. Choose one or more questions to start your day.

Why does _____ easily bring out the best in me?

What might distract me from optimizing _____?

God, what does _____ want to show me about my potential?

CHAPTER 9
Power to Realign

We must look for ways to be an active force in our own lives. We must take charge of our own destinies, design a life of substance and truly begin to live our dreams.
~ Les Brown

Tattooed across the boy's chest were the words, "I am my worst enemy." The message etched upon his skin left a permanent impression on my heart. At an early age, he had already discovered the key to unlock his destiny. Our paths crossed at a basketball fundraiser to help high school students at risk. He told me he got the tattoo after cancer had taken both his mother and aunt, leaving him to survive on his own. He learned to control what he could, his mind. The script on his skin, penned by his heart's desire to thrive, foretold a future of triumph over tribulation.

Each of us is at risk to become our own worst enemy. We judge ourselves harshly with negative self-talk that sabotages our potential. Our doubts derail our dreams and our fears steal our future. Michele, a client who chose the word, freedom, shared how she came to grips with the enemy within.

> "I have been on a journey of 'freedom' this past year and it has been amazing. I realized that what I was really trying to free myself from was my own unrealistic expectations and beating my own self up. I have been trying so many new things as well as reuniting with things I used to love. I took a creative writing class that led to a journaling class that led to a blogging class. I am still not sure

where all of this is leading to but I do feel I am on the right path."

Michele used the power of one word to realign her actions with her passions and most importantly, her current expectations with her desired future.

Scientific Fact

One word can activate the motivational centers of your brain. Research shows when you hold a positive and optimistic word in your mind, you stimulate frontal lobe activity. Your frontal lobe, connected to your motor cortex, moves you into action (*One Word Can Change Your Brain* by Newberg and Waldman).

Additionally, Newberg and Waldman discovered that by focusing on positive words, you change your thalamus, shifting your perception of reality. As your reality shifts, you naturally realign your thoughts, emotions and choices to support your new reality. The veil clouding my vision was lifted after I chose to look at my life through the lens of my one word, awe. As a result, I realigned my thoughts and decisions to experience reverence and wonder throughout each day. I was not disappointed as I began to appreciate and see a whole new world of amazing things!

Spiritual Truth

Adversity is a disorienting wind, shifting your direction and altering the path to your destination. Scripture is replete with verses about God's desire and power to realign our paths.

"The steps of a good man are ordered by the Lord: and he delighteth in his way" (*Psalm 37:23*).

"And thine ears shall hear a word behind thee, saying, This is the way, walk ye in it, when ye turn to the right hand, and when ye turn to the left" (*Isaiah 30:21*).

"This is what the LORD says—your Redeemer, the Holy One of Israel: "I am the LORD your God, who teaches you what is best for you, who directs you in the way you should go" (*Isaiah 48:17 NIV*).

"Trust in the Lord with all thine heart; and lean not unto thine own understanding. In all thy ways acknowledge him, and he shall direct thy paths" (*Proverbs 3:5-6*).

As you veer off course, your one word holds the power to act as a rudder realigning your steps to your destiny. James 3:3-5 explains:

> "When we put bits into the mouths of horses to make them obey us, we can turn the whole animal. Or take ships as an example. Although they are so large and are driven by strong winds, they are steered by a very small rudder wherever the pilot wants to go. Likewise, the tongue is a small part of the body, but

it makes great boasts. Consider what a great forest is set on fire by a small spark. *(NIV)*

Daily Questions to Activate the Power to Realign

Maximize the potential of your one word to realign your actions with your values, dreams and destiny by placing your one word into the blank in each question. Choose one or more questions to start your day.

What direction is _____ taking me in today?

God, why do I easily allow _____ to steer me onto the path you have set before me?

How can I realign my thoughts or actions to express _____ ?

CHAPTER 10
Power to Define

When you come out of the storm, you won't be the same person who walked in. That's what this storm's all about.
~ Haruki Murakami

Mikkal, looking for a new job, was also hungry to "reset, replenish and restore", and "get rid of broken." She was overwhelmed and overly stressed in an unfulfilling leadership position in a large metro Atlanta school district.

Mikkal described herself as a "shrinking violet", a persona developed in childhood. As a young girl, her family moved frequently and she was always the new girl trying to fit in. Her strategy to make friends quickly was not to draw attention to herself. Mikkal started downplaying her talents and strengths, a pattern which followed her into adulthood.

Mikkal chose bloom, a word resonating with her heart's desire to grow a fresh identity. Her word painted a vision of her future self. To create her future, we looked at the qualities of leaders she admired. In a breakthrough moment, she discovered that she already was her ideal leader. Her confidence grew and she no longer called herself a "shrinking violet", but an "impactful, authentic, bold and ground-breaking visionary." Her seeds of identity had sprouted.

She next identified her dream job. Within six months, in a miraculous set of circumstances, Mikkal interviewed for and accepted a position that met all of her criteria. In an unforgettable moment, when she called to share her good news, she declared, "I have bloomed!"

Scientific Fact

Michelle Arbeau, in her book, *The Energy of Words*, demonstrates how to calculate the vibration of a word, cautioning you to use positively charged words to avoid sabotaging your identity. She shares how the trajectory of her life changed when she began to call herself a "celebrity" and not an "intuitive." She offers her testimony, "not to brag, but to show that the power you put behind a word can assist you in manifesting your dreams."

Research from the field of neuroscience proves that our thoughts, emotions and choices changes the structure and function of our brains, making it malleable and adaptable. You contain the power to shape your identity by changing what you say and believe about your current and future potential. Tony Stoltzfus, author of *The Calling Journey* says, "The inability to present yourself as who you are, is a huge obstacle to fulfilling your call."

Spiritual Truth

"The angel of the Lord appeared to him and said to him, 'The Lord is with you, you mighty warrior.' Then the Lord turned to him and said, 'Go in this might of yours and deliver Israel from the hand of Midian; I hereby commission you." Judges 6:12,14

The angel found Gideon threshing wheat in an underground wine-press, hiding from the Midianites. Gideon receives a prophetic word about his identity and destiny when called a mighty warrior. Gideon, blinded by his current qualities and inability to trust God, argues with the Lord, trying to convince him that He has the wrong man! As the story unfolds, Gideon releases his old identity as a fearful farmer, stepping into his new identity as a ferocious fighter.

Scripture specifically instructs us to look at ourselves through the eyes of God who looks at our hearts, not at our outward appearance, to find our identity. (*1Samuel 16:7*) You change your identity through the renewing of your mind, replacing your negativity with words that reveal your hidden potential. (*Ephesians 4:22-24*)

Daily Questions to Activate the Power to Define

Increase the impact of your one word to reveal, restore or strengthen your identity. Place your one word into the blank in each question. Choose one or more questions to start your day.

How can _____ reveal a hidden part of me?

God, how are you going to use _____ today to shape my character?

How can I use _____ today so I am known by my word?

CHAPTER 11

Five Saboteurs and Twelve Activation Strategies

Sow an act and you reap a habit. Sow a habit and you reap a character. Sow a character and you reap a destiny.
~ James Allen

You do not move towards your destiny by simply having a word. While that concept may be obvious to you, I discovered it the hard way – in front of a large group of people. After a client finished endorsing my one word workshop, someone in the crowd hollered out,

"So, what's your word?" She stammered, "I don't remember!"

As soon as you select your one word, like my client, you will face sabotaging forces distracting you from activating your word. I have listed below the five most common saboteurs and twelve activating strategies to optimize your results – and memory!

Saboteur #1: Inconsistent Focus

An irregular focus produces erratic results. A client offers a more creative explanation of this saboteur, "I took my one word home with me and treated it like a stray dog. I sat it in the middle of the room and expected it to do tricks. Nothing happened. I learned that even stray dogs need attention." Maximize the power of your word through consistent, daily practice as you would when building a skill or strengthening a muscle.

Saboteur #2: Focusing on Its Opposite

Your one word has an opposing force fueled by your fears. You find the force by identifying words that are opposite in meaning to your word. For example, a client who chose abundance was afraid of poverty. She chose her word to increase her financial security. She discovered that abundance grew in many areas of her life when she shifted her focus from lack and scarcity, the opposites of abundance, to gratitude.

Fear is a super-charged magnet drawing you toward what you do not want. Whatever you choose to focus upon grows in power, for good or bad. Disarm the opposing force by shifting your attention to the unlimited and life-enriching possibilities your word offers.

Saboteur #3: Let Go of Attachment to Results

While it is wise to have goals and construct a plan of action, it is foolish to believe you can control the course of events. Your word will manifest itself in unpredictable ways through people you have not yet met and events that are unimaginable. Winston Churchill stated, "It is a mistake to look too far ahead. Only one link of the chain of destiny can be handled at a time." Manage your expectations as a football coach handles a real game. Observe the ever-shifting action, keeping a loose grip on your game plan. Remain calm and alert for unexpected developments, appreciating what is unfolding. From that state of detachment, you allow the unexpected and unlimited possibilities to help shape your destiny.

Saboteur #4: Lack of Appreciation

Sandra Anne Taylor, author of *Quantum Success,* says, "According to the Law of Magnetism, your energy of gratitude will only attract more to appreciate in the future." Your abundance increases commensurately with your level of gratitude for what is within and around you. Take time to express gratitude to God for each manifestation of your word, from the tiniest example to the super-sized gift. Your one word contains unlimited gifts, released by the energy of joyous appreciation.

Saboteur #5: Giving Up Too Soon

Getting the most out of your one word takes time, faith and persistency. Nelson Mandela, known as a freedom fighter, did not succumb to opposing forces like jail and slavery. While imprisoned for 27 years, he used his circumstances to develop leadership skills. Thankfully, he persisted, keeping his date with destiny to liberate South Africa. Give your word ample time to take root before you uproot it.

Twelves Strategies to Activate the Power of One Word

Choose any combination of strategies from the menu below. You amplify the power of your word through consistent focus and practice.

1. Identify which of the sixteen desires are the driving forces behind your word. (See page 17) Understanding your desires increases your determination to activate your word. For example, I chose flow, to fulfill my desires for significance and peace.

2. Uncover the full meaning and value of your word.
   Discover the origins of your word as well as its synonyms. I generated this list for awe: goodness, intimacy, wonderment, innocence, purity, magical, reverence, miraculous, tremendousness, numinous, reverence and glory. Your list creates unlimited manifestations of your one word.

3. Make a word collage or visual map.
   One client wrote joy in the middle of a poster board. She added an image that evoked joy along with the following words and phrases: jewels, festivity, shout with joy to God,

pleasure, comfort, rejoice, strength and joy in His presence. Include favorite quotes or scriptures related to your word. To create a word collage, go to www.tagxedo.com and www.wordle.net.

4. Keep your word visible.
   You may find it on a bracelet, necklace, keychain, journal or cup. Create a sign with your word. Write it on a rock or display it on your mirror or screensaver.

5. Listen to a song containing your word for inspiration and motivation.

6. Keep a notebook or journal with quotes or scripture related to your word.

7. Display an inspiring and empowering powerful image that reflects your word.

8. Share your word with your network of friends, family and associates.

    Post it on your social media sites as a way to declare and activate it. Once I started sharing my words, I received support from others who gave me signs, rocks, articles, cups, notecards and even a tote bag with my one word.

9. Memorize scripture related to your one word.

10. Write affirmations or declarations with your one word.

    For example: There is nothing to hold me back from a life of <u>freedom</u> in Christ. The potential for my life is <u>unlimited</u>. I offer <u>unparalleled</u> service at my company.

11. Plant your word in your subconscious each day by asking one or two of the questions found at the end of chapters four through ten.

12. Keep a journal of gratitude for each manifestation of your one word.

    Review your entries from time to time as a way to increase your joy and faith in the seven powers of one word.

Optimize your results by increasing the amount of energy and effort you put into activating the power of your word. You reap what you sow.

CHAPTER 12

Five Stages of Influence

*Destiny is no matter of chance.
It is a matter of choice. It is not a thing
to be waited for, it is a thing to be achieved.*
~ William Jennings Bryan

The trilogy, *Lord of the Rings* by J.R.R. Tolkien, is a spectacular tale of destiny fulfilled. Frodo, a humble hobbit, is charged with saving the inhabitants of Middle Earth. His journey is arduous, filled with adversities that shape and strengthen him. His success hinges on his ability to overcome his own fear and progress through the five stages of influence. In a climactic battle fought at the rim of Mount Doom's volcanic fires, Frodo triumphs over evil to fulfill his destiny.

Looking at Biblical history for a quest of similar magnitude, we find Esther, a Jewish orphan. She lives with her uncle, Mordecai, who serves King Xerxes. Through extraordinary circumstances, King Xerxes selects Esther to replace Vashti, his disobedient wife. When her uncle defies King Xerxes, the king retaliates with a decree to exterminate the Jews. In one of the most inspiring and dramatic appeals that would shape Esther's destiny and an entire nation, Mordecai entreats his niece, "For if you keep silence at such a time as this, relief and deliverance will rise for the Jews from another quarter, but you and your father's family will perish. Who knows? Perhaps you have come to royal dignity for just such a time as this" (*Esther 4:14, NRSV*). Esther's transformation from ragamuffin to royalty positioned her to save a nation. Both Frodo and Esther surrendered to the refining, character-building fires of adversity to optimize their influence and fulfill their destiny.

Like our two heroes, you and your word travel through stages of influence. I credit Leif Heitland, author of *Seeing Through Heaven's Eyes*, for the five stages of growth. They are understanding, value, stewardardship, multiplication and authority.

Your primary objective at stage one, understanding, is to gain knowledge about each of the seven powers. Your deep understanding of the science and the scripture underlying each power provides the confidence and motivation to use your word. Without comprehension, you limit the value of your word.

With understanding, you move to the second stage, value. At a shooting range, I once carelessly held an AK-47 demonstrating my lack of respect for its power. I also scared the daylights out of my son who was standing next to me. When you understand the power and value of a resource, you handle it differently.

At stage three, you become a steward. In Matthew 25:14-30, Jesus shares the Parable of the Talents to relay a strong message about the responsibility of a steward. In the parable, the master who has given three servants varying amounts of money is most displeased with the servant who buries his resources rather than investing them. As a good steward, you consistently invest your time and energy into activating its seven powers.

The fourth stage is multiply. Originally, you may have chosen your word to meet one of your heart's desires or achieve a specific goal. One client chose freedom to help make a career decision and found that freedom expanded to many areas of his life including his relationships, finances and health. Your one word also multiplies by impacting the lives of those around you.

The final stage is authority where your level of influence is at its maximum. Your word becomes an integral part of your identity. When you think of Mother Teresa, what words come to mind? Servant, compassionate, merciful or selfless? All are correct, as Mother Teresa was all of those attributes. You, like her, are respected as the expert or shining example of your word.

Please note that your one word is with you for a season of indefinite length. Some people activate their word for as little as three months and some for a year or more. Your heart combined with your life's experiences will guide you when it is time for a new word.

You are a navigator, weathering the storms of adversity, to fulfill your destiny. Your one word is your light saber, cutting through the darkness of fear. Your one word is your trusted companion, a lifeline when adversity threatens to take you down and out. Your one word rescues and restores you in seven ways. Your one word:

- Orders your chaos
- Nourishes your emotionally and spiritually famished spirit
- Energizes your steps when taking one more seems impossible
- Wakens you to partner with God to conquer fear, doubt and despair
- Optimizes your potential in crises
- Realigns your priorities to conquer confusion and distractions
- Defines your identity aided by the fires of adversity

Adversity presents the opportunity and challenge to dive into your fears and your desires to reveal the one word that is best for you right now. Your one word contains unlimited and unpredictable possibilities for transformation and impact.

My hope is that amidst your hardships and adversity, you enter the doorway to your heart to find your one word nestled deep within. Your heart is ready to release your word and its seven powers into your life, transforming your current circumstances into your destiny.

About the Author

Breast cancer survivor-thriver and founder of Impact Coaching, Susan Brown is a Transformation Strategist and One Word Manifestation Specialist.

Within the last several years, Susan has become synonymous with her immensely popular workshop, *The Power of One Word* which is offered regularly via numerous organizations. She is also one of two certified people in the United States facilitating *Turning Stress into Strength*™, a nationally acclaimed course developed by Brenda Stockdale that boosts the immune system and well-being of those with cancer, chronic illness and chronic stress.

Susan Brown, passionate about growth and learning, holds numerous educational degrees and coaching certifications enabling her to help people transform their suffering and life's challenges into their destiny. She merges the best practices from the fields of psychoneuroimmunology, positive psychology and neuroscience with faith-based principles to help people prosper emotionally, physically and spiritually.

For more information, go to:
www.impactcoaching423.com

CPSIA information can be obtained
at www.ICGtesting.com
Printed in the USA
LVOW04s1102120516
487923LV00017B/169/P